Original title:
Morning Glory Memoirs

Copyright © 2025 Creative Arts Management OÜ
All rights reserved.

Author: Harrison Blake
ISBN HARDBACK: 978-1-80566-650-9
ISBN PAPERBACK: 978-1-80566-935-7

Petals Unfurled

In the garden, a bee does dance,
Tickling petals as if in a trance.
A rooster crows with flair and cheer,
Wait, did I just lose my last beer?

The tulips giggle, the daisies sway,
Who knew flowers could joke this way?
A squirrel steals a sandwich, oh dear!
I swear, my breakfast is not safe here!

Echoes of Daybreak

The sun peeks in, it takes a glance,
A cat on the windowsill starts to prance.
Brewed coffee spills upon my shoe,
Guess it's a morning of slip and woo!

Birds serenade with a chirpy quack,
While I fumble to find my snack.
Is that a shadow or my lost sock?
Laughter erupts as I check the clock!

A Tapestry of Light

In the dawn's glow, the toaster pops,
But my butter just slips and flops.
Breakfast wants to stage a show,
As I juggle my eggs like a pro!

Sunlight spills like melted cheese,
A dance floor for ants, oh how they tease!
A coffee cup, a whirling breeze,
I smile at chaos, my heart at ease.

Sunbeams and Shadows

With a wink, the sun waves high,
While I squint up at the blue sky.
Lost shoes stumble on the lawn,
I laugh, for my morning's almost gone!

A dog trots by with a silly grin,
Chasing the shade that's wearing thin.
I chase my dreams like a runaway kite,
In this circus of mornings, all feels right!

Underneath the Rising Sun

Birds are chirping, what a fuss,
Coffee brewing in a rush.
Socks mismatched, oh what a sight,
Dancing shadows, morning light.

Pancakes flipping, syrup spills,
Half of it all, give me thrills.
Cat is pouncing, what a game,
Chasing sunbeams, who's to blame?

Shoes untied, hair a mess,
Who needs grooming? No distress.
Joggers pass with looks bemused,
My morning laughter, quite infused.

Chasing remnants of sweet dreams,
Seagulls squawking, burst of screams.
Day is wild, unleash the fun,
Underneath this rising sun.

Embraced by Light

Sunrise tickles, bright and bold,
Pajamas still, the chill, I'm told.
Toast is burning, smoke's a sign,
Breakfast battles, ever divine.

My dog leaps with morning glee,
Catching rays that chase the tree.
Neighbors peek with amused smiles,
As I wrestle with my tiles.

Coffee spills, it stains my shirt,
Bumbling feet make bending hurt.
Laughter echoes, joy's the key,
In this light, I'm wild and free.

A sloth-like dance, my very best,
Embraced by warmth, I yearn for rest.
A glorious start, hilarity reigns,
In this chaos, bliss retains.

A Day's Soft Prelude

Sunlight tiptoes, kisses cheeks,
Snooze alarms? Oh, such peaks.
Pajama-clad, I rule the house,
Cats and coffee, playing mouse.

Butterflies flit, outside my door,
And I stumble, looking for more.
Toast on the floor, bread's gone rogue,
Laughter beckons like a vogue.

Neighbors gossip, as I prance,
Wobbling, tripping, my goofy dance.
Time to shine, what a rare feat,
Mirth and blunders, life's bittersweet.

Muffins laugh, they puff and rise,
A cheerful chaos fills the skies.
This prelude starts with jiggles and laughs,
In every moment, joy soon halves.

Horizon's Promise

Sunbeams stretch upon the dawn,
A sleepy yawn, then I'm withdrawn.
Socks invade, they spark delight,
Scavenging treasures, a silly sight.

Butterflies flutter, friends unite,
My hair's a mess, a furry fright.
Juggling toast, I try to mend,
In this circus, laughter's the trend.

Chasing shadows, butterflies fly,
A froggy leap, oh me, oh my!
Neighbors chuckle, what a scene,
In this daydream, laughter's queen.

Time unfolds, oh what a tease,
A playful breeze that aims to please.
With smiles wrapped like sunny threads,
Horizon's promise, joy spreads.

Dawn's Quiet Revelations

The rooster crows, a clumsy start,
He thinks he's Mozart, playing art.
Coffee brews with splatters loud,
As sleepy dreams tiptoe, unbowed.

Socks mismatched, a fashion crime,
In the mirror, I ponder time.
Toast pops up, a bread surprise,
Jams on my face, oh, what a rise!

Sunlight spills like orange juice,
My cat thinks it's a wild moose.
She chases shadows with such grace,
While I trip over my own space.

With every giggle, morning stirs,
In this chaos, peace occurs.
Life's a circus, and I laugh,
In dawn's light, I find my path.

Skylines Bathed in Gold

The sun creeps in with golden gleam,
Painting rooftops, what a dream!
Frogs in the yard can't find their shoes,
They croak in chorus, sharing news.

Birds take flight with socks on beaks,
They steal my breakfast, oh the freaks!
While I chase them, slipped on a rug,
Laughter bubbles; life's a mug.

Clouds become bunnies, oh how they play,
Bouncing high in a silly ballet.
Scooters whiz by with kids in tow,
Faces painted bright, putting on a show.

With every grin, the city's alive,
Sidewalk cafes, where giggles thrive.
Morning skips like a pebble tossed,
In the gold of dawn, no joys lost.

Flickers of Dawn

As the world stirs, my slippers roam,
Chasing dust bunnies in our home.
Fridge magnets dance, a silly scene,
Breakfast waits, smelling like whipped cream.

By the window, a squirrel performs,
Collecting acorns, he breaks norms.
I sip my coffee and laugh out loud,
How did he think he's so proud?

A sock puppet battle brews in the warm,
While my plants decide to underperform.
Toast pops up with a little cheer,
Crispy smiles, can't help but sneer.

The clock ticks down like a timer set,
For the fun of morning, I won't forget.
In the flicker of light, my quirks appear,
With every chuckle, the day draws near.

A Symphony of Awakening

Alarm clock sings a silly song,
Telling me sleep isn't quite wrong.
But the bed begs me to stay put,
While my coffee pot starts to toot.

Outfit clashes like colors in paint,
Tomorrow's fashion, oh how quaint.
The dog wears my hat, he's quite a sight,
And prances around, full of delight.

Birds in the trees add to the mix,
With tweets and chirps, a comedy fix.
I pull on socks and head out the door,
Only to find I've worn one more.

Sunshine filters through the air,
Sweet chaos, the world's a fair.
In this symphony, laughter rings,
As morning's baton conducts with flings.

The Tenderness of Twilights Past

In pajamas up to my knees,
I search for my socks with great ease.
Coffee spills on my shirt, oh dear,
As I dance like no one's near.

The cat stares at me with disdain,
While I juggle my toast, it's insane!
Butter flies like a bird in the sky,
I should probably just say goodbye.

The sun peeks in, oh what a sight,
I squint and mutter, 'Not yet, not quite!'
With a yawn and a stretch, I plot my course,
To conquer the day with minimal force.

Yet laughter escapes as I trip on a shoe,
In this wobbly dance, who knew?
Twilight may be tender, yet we laugh,
As I sip my coffee, take a photograph!

Awakening in Color.

The rooster crows like a broken toy,
I wake up ready to bring some joy.
My toothbrush rebels and jumps away,
As I negotiate with it each day.

Sunlight bursts in, a vibrant hue,
While I search for breakfast, what to chew?
A pot of cereal, two cups is a riot,
The kitchen's a mess, but who wants to try it?

I dress in stripes that clash with my mood,
Confetti on me, oh, isn't that rude?
Outside, the world is a carnival bright,
Where every little mishap feels just right.

Yet in this mayhem, joy starts to bloom,
As I trip on the dog, who claims my room.
Awakening in colors of whimsy and cheer,
Life in its chaos feels so very clear.

Awakening Dreams

I roll out of bed like a tumbleweed,
Pajamas as my armor, no need to plead.
The mirror screams at my bedhead hair,
While I ponder the magic of daily fare.

Coffee brews a tune of jazz so sweet,
As I shuffle around, discovering my feet.
The toast pops up as if to declare,
'You can do this, just don't lose your flair!'

The cat prances by like a furry ghost,
While I contemplate breakfast as utmost.
With a splash of milk, and a wink of fate,
I scoop up my cereal, feeling first-rate.

From dreams I emerge, a comical sight,
In the theater of morning, everything's light.
Awakening dreams in the laughter we share,
Life's a party – just stop and beware!

Dawn's Gentle Whisper

Dawn creeps in like a ticklish cat,
With shades of orange and perfect chat.
I sip my coffee, pretending to think,
As the toast starts dancing on the brink.

Outside, the birds break into song,
While I rummage for clothes all wrong.
The sock monster strikes yet again,
In this daily war, I cannot pretend.

The sun winks at me, a mischievous tease,
As I negotiate breakfast like it's a breeze.
Honey spills like a golden stream,
This kitchen chaos feels like a dream.

Yet laughter bubbles like the morning dew,
As I spill juice, and the cat looks askew.
In dawn's gentle whisper, I find my way,
Embracing the funny in every new day.

Blossoms of Renewal

The rooster crows, a wake-up call,
Eggs are cracking, can't drop the ball.
Coffee spills, oh what a mess!
Who needs sleep when you've got stress?

Socks mismatched, a fashion crime,
Running late, what a waste of time!
Pancakes flip, but land on the floor,
Laugh it off; who could ask for more?

Cats are chasing the morning light,
Dogs just bark, what a silly sight.
Birds are singing, off-key, it seems,
Life is perfect, or so it beams!

So here's to mornings, wild and bright,
Filled with laughter from dawn till night.
Though chaos reigns in every zone,
These joyful blunders feel like home.

Daybreak Diaries

The sun peeks in, a golden beam,
But sleep calls loudly, a comfy dream.
Brush your teeth, don't skip the chore,
You might scare folks right out the door!

Frogs are croaking in morning's light,
Claiming their fame like it's a fight.
Toast pops up, and what a cheer,
Charred and crispy, a breakfast smear!

Chasing the cat, she jumps and plays,
Knocking over everything in her ways.
Coffee's hot, but spills down the side,
Mornings like these are quite the ride!

Journals open, writing scenes galore,
With each outburst, we laugh and roar.
A day begins with humor in store,
The tales of dawn leave us wanting more.

Sunbeam Stories

Sunbeams dance on the window's ledge,
Time to wake up, we'll surely pledge.
Yoga mat's hiding beneath the bed,
But who needs calm when you can spread?

Cereal spills like glittering snow,
Spoon upside down? Yes, that's the flow.
Pajamas still on, and that's just fine,
The world outside keeps asking, "Why dine?"

Neighbors' dogs tend to start a rave,
While I just clumsily attempt to wave.
Knock, knock jokes are the morning spree,
Laughter's the best, absolutely free!

So here we are, with sunshine bright,
Collecting stories that bring delight.
In every chuckle, in every cheer,
Morning fun is what we hold dear.

The Fresh Start Chronicles

New day dawns, a fresh new start,
But where's my shoe? It's quite the art.
Coffee's brewing, at last, a beam,
Just kidding! I forgot the cream!

The toast is singing, a burnt duet,
Blackened edges? You can bet!
A quick run to the store for a fix,
And dodge the carts, oh what a mix!

Kids are bouncing, running around,
Pajamas on display, joy abound.
Who needs rules when the giggles fly?
In these fresh starts, we learn to fly!

So here we sit, a motley crew,
With our tales and mischief all so true.
Laughter resounds, it's what we crave,
Embracing life, we joyfully wave.

Dawn's Gentle Whispers

The rooster crows, oh what a sound,
As sleepy heads spin round and round.
Coffee brews a bitter song,
While toast pops up, the wait feels long.

Socks grow legs and dance around,
Under the bed, they can't be found.
Brush in hand, we paint our faces,
Hoping to dodge the morning races.

A cat on the windowsill takes flight,
Confusing birds with her morning fright.
A squirrel steals all the garden snacks,
While I chase after him, no time to relax!

Laughter echoes through the mist,
In this crazy dawn, I can't resist.
With sleepy dreams out on display,
Who knew mornings could be this way?

Awakening Petals

As sunlight creeps in through the shade,
I squint my eyes, the light's a trade.
The alarm clock sings a silly tune,
While I ponder breakfast with a cartoon.

Waking blooms in the flower bed,
Whispering secrets I must be fed.
Pancakes flip in a stylish ballet,
Twirling syrup, come what may!

Birds gossip above in a comical choir,
As I trip on my shoelace and retire.
A bear in pajamas roams the hall,
Good luck, dear morning, after all!

With laughter mingling in the air,
These funny moments are beyond compare.
So let the petals flutter free,
In a world that's silly as can be!

First Light Chronicles

In the hush of dawn, the toaster sings,
While dreams take flight on laughter's wings.
I spill my juice, oh what a sight,
As the cat takes off in pure delight.

Coffee brews like a bubbling queen,
With thrilling aromas and caffeine sheen.
Mismatched socks start their daily dance,
As I stumble through my morning chance.

The mirror cracks a joke, I grin,
Choosing the hint of chaos within.
To the fridge I go, a grand parade,
Selecting snacks—who needs charades?

In this chapter of morning strife,
Each giggle carves a joyful life.
With mischief in the air we play,
First light sparks, come what may!

Sunlit Remembrances

Oh sunlit beams, a raucous laugh,
Turning my cereal into a bath.
The dog steals my toast, with charm and grace,
While I chase him down—oh, what a race!

The calendar shouts with its bright design,
Reminding me of my tasks, how divine!
Sticky notes litter the table wide,
Like clue-filled treasures, I must abide.

Out the window, the world is spry,
With joggers leaping as I sigh.
But who needs exercise, anyway?
When my morning could be a comedy play!

So let us revel in this happy scene,
With foibles and fun, a daily routine.
Each giggle a memory to hold onto tight,
Sunlit moments that make everything bright!

A Curtain of Light

The sun peeks in with a wink,
Cats yawn loud, much to their link.
Coffee brews with a playful cheer,
While toast dances like it's in a theater.

Socks mismatched, a fashion faux pas,
I trip over my pet, a tiny fur ball.
The dog chases shadows in the hall,
While I laugh hard, might just fall.

Birds gossip from a branch so high,
While I contemplate my pancake pie.
The fridge hums a delightful tune,
As I dance alone, waking up too soon.

Sunrise grins with a cheeky beam,
Turning everyday chaos into a dream.
Life starts fresh with a joyful spin,
Oh, how delightful this state I'm in!

Dreams that Awaken

A thought floats in, it's quite absurd,
Why was I chased by a singing bird?
The alarm bell rings, what a silly sound,
As I leap from bed, my socks unbound.

Mismatched shoes on my eager feet,
I slip and slide, oh what a feat!
The cereal's gone, only crumbs remain,
Yet the laughter sparks, a sweet refrain.

Outside the window, kids skip and play,
While I pretend it's my birthday today.
Life's a parade of quirky sights,
A carnival ride filled with joyous flights.

Dreams of a dragon and flying cheese,
Make mornings feel like a summer breeze.
Here's to the fun, the silly, the strange,
In this waking world, where laughter can change!

The Glow of Promise

Sunlight spills like juice on the floor,
It tickles me, who could ask for more?
The toast pops up, a little too high,
It lands on my nose, oh me, oh my!

Socks march in with a flapping grace,
As I chase them down in a funny race.
The cat rolls over, a fluffball of fluff,
And I can't help laughing, oh isn't it tough?

My coffee spills, a caffeinated art,
On the floor, it twirls, a wild heart.
The news laughs too, strange things abound,
Mornings here are joyfully profound.

A promise shines in the day's soft glow,
As I wander where the giggles flow.
With every hiccup and silly dance,
Life is a game, come take a chance!

Sunrise Melodies

The rooster sings, but off-key it seems,
While I hum along with my half-formed dreams.
The sun stretches wide, yawning bright,
It spills golden laughter in morning light.

The pancakes flip with an acrobatic flair,
While I chase after my wild, frizzy hair.
The neighbor's cat gives me a disapproving stare,
As I juggle eggs in the fun morning air.

My toast plays pop music, it's a hot jam,
While I do the dance of a goofy glam.
The chocolate milk pours with a splashy thrill,
As breakfast becomes a clumsy thrill.

Oh, morning's song is a bubbly tune,
It dances with joy from dawn till noon.
With each unexpected, silly surprise,
Life's sweetest joys are in the sunrise!

Sunrise Sketches

The rooster crows, a funny sound,
My coffee spills upon the ground.
The sun peeks in with a cheeky grin,
A brand-new day for all to win.

I trip on shoes that don't fit right,
Chasing the cat in morning light.
The toast pops up, it's burned, oh dear,
Laughing as I choke down my cheer.

The socks don't match, but who will see?
Dancing round, so carelessly.
A toast to blunders, that's my art,
In this bright day, I play my part.

So here's my sketch, a wobbly start,
Morning antics, let's all take part.
Laughter blooms like flowers, bright,
In this sunrise scene, pure delight.

The Nurturing Light

The sun yawns wide, the day begins,
As ducks parade, in silly spins.
My plant is shriveling; poor little sprout,
Gave it a drink, it's all but out!

The toaster fights, it pops in rage,
Bread flies out, like a tiny page.
I catch it mid-air, what a surprise,
It lands right here with winking eyes.

The morning light hugs all it sees,
Caressing trees with playful breeze.
Every shadow's a humorous face,
Nature's sketches in a lively race.

With laughter, I sip my joyful brew,
A day to cherish, bright and new.
In sunshine's glow, let's all unite,
With funny twists and warmth so bright.

Rebirth in Bloom

In the garden, blooms awake,
Butterflies dance; for goodness' sake!
Tulips giggle in hues so bold,
They whisper secrets, stories told.

The bees all buzz, but what's the rush?
Fuzzy creatures in a morning hush.
I tried to join, but slipped and fell,
Into the flowers, oh well, oh well!

The sun's a painter, strokes so carefree,
Each petal shines, a jubilee.
Best buds share a laugh, a crinkle or two,
In this blooming world, anything will do!

The fresh new day is here to stay,
Let's celebrate in a silly way.
With flowers twirling, dreams anew,
Laughter blooms in every hue.

A Symphony of Daybreak

The dawn sings out, a funny tune,
The squirrels dance, a morning boon.
I trip on grass, take a deep breath,
In this symphony, embrace sweet theft.

Chirping birds, they squawk and play,
Scaring my cat, who runs away.
Leaves rustle in this lively show,
A concert where the best bits flow.

Coffee's brewing, that rich aroma,
Turns my kitchen into a zona.
Espresso spills, oh what a scene,
A jester's chaos in a coffee machine.

Laughter echoes, bright and light,
In this day's mosaic, pure delight.
With every note, let's sing along,
In this cheerful dawn, we belong.

Petals and Promises

In the garden with blooms so bright,
A bee stole my toast, what a sight!
I laughed at the bud, a prankster's jest,
Nature's comedy always the best.

A squirrel wore a hat made of leaves,
Dancing like mad, pulling at sleeves.
Promises whispered with giggles around,
Where joy in the petals is utterly found.

With every bloom, a wink and a tease,
Petals falling down like sneezes with ease.
The sun peeks high, blushing with glee,
Nature's own prank, just wait and see!

So here's to the laughs that flowers can bring,
With petals that chuckle, it's springtime's fling.
Keep frolicking on, my dear friend of mine,
In this garden of giggles where we all dine.

Memories Beneath the Rising Sun

Fizzing like soda, the sun pops awake,
A toast to the toast that I burned in the bake.
Chasing my shadow, I trip on the lawn,
A dance with the grass, from dusk till the dawn.

Squirrels debate if my hat's a ripe fruit,
And I yell at a bird who's stealing my flute.
Memories simmer in shadows that play,
While laughter tickles in a silly ballet.

Under the sky, my thoughts take a flight,
The sun's shining bright, what a glorious sight!
A hiccup of joy, the morning unfolds,
While tales of mishaps are quietly told.

So raise up your coffee, let's toast to the day,
With silly adventures just a splash away.
Each memory shines like a spark in the sun,
In this giggling dance, life's just begun!

Light's Embrace

Sunbeams are wigglin', tickling my face,
Caught in the sun's warm, delightful embrace.
I slipped on my slippers, one big, then one small,
And laughed till I cried as I started to fall.

A cat with a crown sits plotting his scheme,
While birds tweet their gossip, caught up in a dream.
With ruffled-up feathers, they strut and they sway,
A royal parade in the morning's ballet.

Golden rays wink as they peek through the trees,
Where mischief and magic drift on the breeze.
Moments of joy in this kooky delight,
All wrapped up snug in soft morning light.

So come join the fun, in this world bright and bold,
With laughs that are forever, and stories retold.
In light's gentle arms, we stumble and glide,
With smiles on our faces, let's enjoy the ride!

The Morning's Lullaby

The rooster sings loud, he thinks he's a star,
While I wrestle pillows, where did my dreams spar?
In the chaos of dawn, with a yawning parade,
I fight with my blanket, all logic betrayed.

Coffee's in battle with a sleepy-eyed grin,
As I ponder the wonders of where to begin.
The cat's juggle's my sock, what does he expect?
A thief in the night, oh, what a neglect!

With giggles of dawn, sunbeams start to sway,
As I trip over slippers and fail at ballet.
Each chuckle resounds like a cheerful refrain,
In the symphony sung by my morning's campaign.

Let's lift up our spirits, join in a dance,
For life's an adventure, let's give it a chance.
With laughter as music, we'll sing with delight,
In this quirky adventure, everything feels right!

Elysium in the Morning

Roosters crow, my alarm's on strike,
Dreams were wild, oh what a hike!
Coffee beans dance, in rhythmic sway,
Morning antics begin to play.

Toast pops up, like a golden prize,
Butter slides down, oh what a surprise!
Cat plays judge as I spill the tea,
Laughter bubbles, has to be free.

Socks mismatched, but who really cares?
Hair like a bird's, wild in the air!
Breakfast chaos, spilling milk galore,
Start the day off with a side of uproar.

Embrace the hustle, the silly, the fun,
Life's a circus, and we've just begun!
With giggles and grins, we're off to explore,
Elysium calls, who could ask for more?

The Awakening Sun

The sun peeks in, a cheeky grin,
Yawning loudly, the day begins.
Pajamas fly, a fashion spree,
Out to the world, here comes me!

Cereal spills like a waterfall,
Milk makes waves, oh what a brawl!
Dogs prance around, ready to play,
Life's a party, come join the sway.

Balancing breakfast while texting friends,
Promises of fun, the day transcends.
Shoes on wrong, but who gives a hoot?
A wild style, all crazy and cute.

Tickle the sun, let adventure unfurl,
Dance with the day, give it a whirl!
With laughter as fuel, we'll soar and run,
Embracing the joy of the waking sun!

A Journal of Sunlit Moments

Pen in hand, my notes go wild,
Recalling antics, oh what a child!
Spilled juice, a colorful crime,
Each little blunder, sincerely sublime.

First sip of coffee, lips on fire,
Burned my tongue, oh what a liar!
Fried eggs dance as they splatter and leap,
Chasing the cat, now that's a heap!

Wrote down dreams of flying high,
Reality check—I'm stuck, oh my!
Scrambled thoughts, and calendar flips,
Lost in giggles, tough not to trip.

Memories glow in the morning light,
With laughter echoing, all feels right.
Each moment cherished, we'll proudly boast,
Sunlit snippets, oh how we toast!

Light Upon the Horizon

Light spills forth like a painter's brush,
Hues of gold in a glorious rush.
Birds chirp tunes, let's join in the play,
Laughter echoing, come what may!

Socks in the air, not quite on my feet,
Chasing my coffee, a daring feat.
Pancakes flipping, they soar like a kite,
Dropping them all, a true morning fright.

Garden gnomes giggle, their faces aglow,
Witnessing chaos, just so you know.
A wave to the mailman, who knows my routine,
With smiles exchanged, it's a world so keen.

Embrace this madness, this wild, fun spree,
With light upon horizons, we're happy and free.
Striking a pose in the soft morning air,
Life's a circus, with wonders to spare!

Dew-Kissed Dreams

The sun peeks in, a cheeky grin,
The cat yells 'breakfast' from the bin.
My pajamas shorts are mismatched pairs,
I trip over shoes, forget my cares.

A coffee spill, oh what a sight,
The mug's a dancer in morning light.
I catch a squirrel with a brow raised high,
He steals my toast and waves goodbye.

The clock ticks loud, it mocks my pace,
While toothpaste ends up on my face.
I've brushed away yesterday's mess,
But my hair's a monument to distress.

Yet through the chaos, laughter rolls,
Each blunder a tale that fills my soul.
With dew-kissed dreams on wobbly feet,
Life's morning circus can't be beat.

The Aroma of Beginning

The kettle sings, a bird in flight,
I dream of donuts, soft and light.
But moments later, who could guess?
I've brewed a potion of coffee stress.

The fridge, a treasure hunt gone wrong,
Finds leftover pizza—still strong!
Each bite is magic, a funky tune,
I dance with breakfast on a broom.

The toast pops up with a little shout,
It's half-a-burn, but there's no doubt.
But nothing can beat this crazy cheer,
Where every mishap brings good beer.

So laughter blooms in the morning light,
With every flavor, pure delight.
I'll take a sip, I'll take a chance,
In this odd routine, I find my dance.

Hues of Hope

The sunrise paints with colors bright,
Awakening dreams from the night.
I step outside, one shoe astray,
A tiny bird laughs, 'that's quite the way!'

I dive for daffodils, vibrant and bold,
But step on a slug – oh, tales untold!
With each little slip, the giggles grow,
A canvas of chaos, the perfect show.

Neighbors wave, their dogs take flight,
One steals my hat — oh, what a sight!
With hues of hope and giggles galore,
This morning's a masterpiece to adore.

My heart's a palette of whimsy and zest,
Chasing the sunrise, I feel so blessed.
In oh-so-funny, colorful cheer,
Each day is a canvas; let's revere!

Echoes of Early Bliss

The rooster crows—a clumsy start,
He missed the mark, bless his heart.
I fumble with eggs, they slip and flop,
Roll off the counter, a breakfast drop!

A dog barks loudly, claiming the prize,
As bacon waves, a greasy surprise.
I laugh at my kitchen, a war zone now,
Yet somehow it feels like a sacred vow.

The radio plays an old-time tune,
As I chase my dreams with a wooden spoon.
But syrup drips like tears of joy,
While pancakes spin like they're a toy.

With echoes of laughter bouncing about,
I dance like no one's watching, no doubt.
My morning saga, a glorious twist,
Filled with bliss that cannot be missed.

Daybreak's Canvas

The sun peeks out, a cheeky grin,
Coffee spills with a playful spin,
Socks mismatched, a fashion spree,
Birds serenade, oh what glee!

Pancakes fly, they make a leap,
While toast decides it's time to sleep,
The cat is plotting, just you see,
A breakfast heist, oh where's the tea?

The morning rush, a wild chase,
A race against the time and space,
With toothpaste smears and joyful shouts,
Who needs calm? It's what life's about!

So here's to dawn, with its quirky charm,
With laughter and chaos, it brings no harm,
A canvas bright, with splashes bold,
A jolly tale that's waiting to be told.

Radiant Reflections

Reflections in the window glow,
A sleepy head with hair in tow,
Mirror laughs at my wild style,
I chuckle back, it's worth my while.

Socks still lost, oh where'd they roam?
To adventures far from our home,
A cereal box, with promises bright,
Turns out they dance at breakfast light.

I trip on shoes tossed in a heap,
The day begins with a silly leap,
As I chase down that rogue toast slice,
With giggles and grumbles, oh so nice!

Each reflection tells a funny tale,
Of quirky moments that never pale,
And as the sun shines, I can't refrain,
From laughter that dances in my brain.

The Blooming Day's Tale

The flowers yawn to greet the morn,
While bees wear tiny hats, quite worn,
A butterfly swoops in for a chat,
As squirrels grumble, "Where's my hat?"

The garden's filled with silly sights,
A gnome debates the bird in flight,
A rabbit jokes, "Is that a bloom?"
As daisies giggle, free of gloom.

The sun spills juice across the lawn,
While neighbors ponder if they're drawn,
To join the fun or stand aloof,
With smiles and chuckles, we find the proof!

So here's to blooms that tell a tale,
Of wacky days that never pale,
With humor stitched in morning's glow,
A blooming day is ours to show!

Glimmers of Yesteryear

In the attic lies a dusty trunk,
Full of toys and socks that stunk,
I sift through memories, lost in time,
Oh what fun, each quirky rhyme!

A teddy bear with no one to hug,
While jumping jacks dance, a bit snug,
The memories twirl like autumn leaves,
With laughter sticking to the eaves.

Old photos showing faces bright,
With goofy grins and sheer delight,
The same old jokes still laugh aloud,
In this cozy, clear-eyed crowd.

So I gather these glimmers near,
Each silly moment, loud and clear,
A jest from yesteryear brings cheer,
As the heart's laughter draws us near.

The Soft Unfolding

In the early light, the roosters crow,
A chicken wearing socks, what a show!
Coffee spills like morning dew,
While cats plot their escape from view.

Socks don't match, but who really cares?
A pancake lands on a lady's hair!
The toast pops up, a jumpy dance,
And the dog stumbles, lost in a trance.

Butterflies chase the buzzing bees,
As the toast burns with a loud sneeze!
The kids rush out, with mismatched shoes,
Who knew mornings had so many hues?

Laughter spills, a bright cacophony,
In this circus, we find harmony!
From sleepyheads, to giggles, so spry,
What a way to greet the sky!

A Light Through the Mist

Cereal floats like boats on milk,
The cat surveys, all smooth as silk.
Fog rolls in, then rolls away,
A pancake toss? Someone's gonna pay!

Hats are worn at a silly angle,
As the kids bicker over the jangle.
Mom's new recipe's a tad too bright,
"Is that a cake, or a disco light?"

The dog has snuck off with the bread,
While visions of butter dance in his head.
A squirrel shouts, "You're all so slow!"
Yet they're running late, as they always go.

Magic awaits past the misty haze,
With giggles erupting in funny displays!
Through chaos, the sunlight spills,
A morning of mischief that always thrills!

Radiant Beginnings

Sunshine peeks, a golden eye,
Pajamas spotted, oh my, oh my!
Caffeine hugs the sleepy soul,
As cereal fills every bowl.

The dog prances, all proud and bold,
With socks in his mouth, quite the hold!
Silly socks, the fashion king,
He struts around, ready to sing!

Kids tumble down the stairs like logs,
Chasing shadows and a host of frogs.
An orange peel, a slip and slide,
"Who's the fastest?" became the pride.

Twirling in sunlight, laughter spreads,
As pancakes flip off sleepy heads!
Morning's chaos, a joyful scene,
In this world, we're all a team!

The Spirit of the Break of Day

As dawn breaks through with a sneaky grin,
A bagel rolls like it's trying to win.
Sipping tea, the kettle sings,
Meanwhile, the cat's up to all sorts of things.

The toast yells out, "I'm quite a catch!"
While kids argue, "You're just a batch!"
A rogue muffin does a dance,
Flipping its lid, it takes a chance!

Outside, the squirrels throw an affair,
With acorns bouncing everywhere.
The sun beams down, in quite a cheer,
While breakfast turns to giggles here.

Bouncing out the door, all joy and glee,
What will we find? Just wait and see!
For in this mirth, we've found our way,
Capturing the spirit of a playful day!

Hues of Hope at Dawn

A rooster crows, the day has come,
Cats stretch wide, the world feels fun.
Coffee brews with fragrant grace,
Socks mismatched, a silly race.

Birds chirp loud in blithe delight,
Sunshine fights to claim the light.
A squirrel dances on a tree,
While I trip on my cup of tea.

Neighbors wave, then quickly hide,
In pajamas as they bide.
Who would think this morning scene,
Could spark laughter, bright and keen?

With toast and jam, I stake my claim,
To breakfast bliss, a quirky game.
It's dawn again, oh what a start,
Life unfolds, a work of art.

Sunlit Echoes of Yesterday

Yesterday's cereal stuck in my teeth,
I laugh aloud, no hint of grief.
Life rolls on in playful ways,
Mismatched shoes, forgotten days.

The sun peeks through the window's seams,
Chasing away the last of dreams.
A spoon dances like it's in a show,
But I just stare, where did it go?

The cat's on guard, a mighty queen,
Pouncing on dust, so sly and keen.
"Don't mind me," she seems to say,
"Your clumsiness brightens the day!"

As shadows stretch their lazy feet,
I juggle oranges, feel the heat.
Still laughing at yesterday's mess,
For in these moments, I feel blessed.

A Dance with the Dawn

The clock alarm sings off-key fun,
A choreographed dance has begun.
Slippers glide across the floor,
As I pirouette to the kitchen door.

Eggs start to sizzle, a lyrical sound,
Spatula twirls, flipping joy around.
The dog joins in, with a howling cheer,
Tails wagging wildly, no fear here.

Balloons float in my morning thought,
What a joy these small things brought.
I spill the juice, it splashes high,
Our laughter rings as it dances by.

So here I twirl, a morning mess,
In this wild little dance, I feel blessed.
With each sip of joy, it's clear to see,
Each morning holds a bit of glee.

The Palette of Awakening

Colors spill from the sun's bright tray,
A brush of laughter guides the way.
Pajamas painted with last night's views,
Who needs canvas? I've got these shoes!

Bacon crisping in the pan, a tease,
"Come on, breakfast! Please, oh please!"
But the toast jumps and does a flip,
While I prepare my morning trip.

Outside, the garden blooms with flair,
A butterfly lands, without a care.
The morning eye, a painter's wish,
I reach for coffee, a perfect dish.

A swipe of laughter fills the air,
Each sip and smile without a care.
In this palette of the day, I find,
Life is art, and it's feeling kind.

The Awakening Heart

The alarm clock screams, what a surprise,
My dreams still dancing in my eyes.
With hair like a bird's nest in flight,
I navigate mornings, a comical sight.

Coffee spills like a morning flood,
I try to sip, but it's more like mud.
Toast does the tango, bread in a spin,
Breakfast is chaos; where do I begin?

The cat looks at me, judging my moves,
As I trip on shoes, oh, the daily grooves.
Mirror reflects a bewildered soul,
Yet laughter ignites, that's the morning goal.

So here I stand, with jumbled glee,
Taking on dawn like it's chasing me.
Life starts anew with each silly part,
Embracing the chaos, the awakening heart.

A Journey Through Morning Dew

Out in the garden, what do I see?
Dew on the lilies, a sparkly spree.
The hose is tangled, I dance with glee,
Squirting myself, now I'm as wet as can be!

The sun peeks out, a shy little guy,
I wave at the clouds as they float by.
A squirrel steals berries, oh what a thief,
While I try to capture every leaf.

Butterflies flutter like they own the show,
Chasing them wildly, to and fro.
I trip on a root, down I go in a huff,
Laughter erupts; mornings are tough!

Yet up I get, with a laugh and a spin,
The day is young; let the adventure begin.
With joy in my heart, and a skip in my shoe,
Life's a grand journey through morning dew.

Golden Horizons

Golden rays spill as the curtains toss,
I blink at the brightness, oh what a loss!
Pajamas still clinging, my hair in a mess,
Can this be called fashion? I guess, I confess.

Breakfast calls, but first, I protest,
Is it too early for caffeine fest?
The toast pops up like a jack-in-the-box,
Burnt to a crisp, like my lucky socks.

A dance with the coffee, a spill on the floor,
Who knew one cup could lead to such war?
Yet laughter erupts, as I scoff and twist,
Embracing the mayhem, I can't resist.

As day stretches wide like a cat's lazy yawn,
I'll chase after dreams 'til the first light is gone.
With giggles and joy, and a flip of my hair,
I greet golden horizons, shedding my care.

The First Breath of Day

With a yawn that echoes, the day comes alive,
Dust bunnies scatter; they plot and they thrive.
The sun gives a wink, the sky's in a glow,
But here on my pillow, I'm moving so slow.

The dog brings a ball, a slobbery tease,
As I fumble for socks; I'm not yet at ease.
My toast does a flip, the butter slides free,
Mornings like this, oh, such comedy!

Joggers zoom past, fit as a beam,
While I trudge along, still lost in a dream.
A squirrel gives chase, thinking I'm prey,
Together we laugh; it's quite the ballet!

Yet here I stand, with a grin on my face,
Finding joy hidden in this silly race.
With each little quirk, the dawn starts to play,
Celebrating the whimsy—the first breath of day.

A Tincture of Dawn

The rooster crows, but still I snooze,
A sock on my foot, the other one loose.
Coffee brews, it's a wild chase,
Tripping over the cat, oh what a race!

Sunlight peeks through the curtain's fold,
My hair's a mess, but I'm feeling bold.
The toast pops up, it's burnt to a crisp,
I grin and confess, it was quite the lisp!

With cereal scattered across the floor,
I laugh at the chaos, oh, there's always more.
A dance with a broom, a sweep and a sway,
Morning giggles chase my worries away!

The clock ticks loudly, I'm late once more,
But first, let me take a moment to score.
A day to begin with joyous delight,
With all of this fun, everything feels right!

The Light that Beckons

Chirp, chirp, chirp, the birds sing along,
I'm tangled in sheets, where's my morning song?
I hop from the bed, land flat on the floor,
The slippers I wore are now missing in war!

The sun winks at me from behind the trees,
I trip on a toy, 'Oh, sweet heavens, please!'
A brush with the mirror reflects a wild face,
I laugh at the spirit of this silly race.

A quick sip of juice, I'm saving the day,
The kitchen's a mess, in a colorful way.
With sprinkles of laughter and sunshine bright,
This quirky morning feels just so right!

I grab my keys, and I'm ready to bolt,
But phew! I forgot my lucky cat's coat.
With a wink and a grin, I dash out the door,
Today's going to shine, like it's never before!

Brushed by the Day

Awake with a stretch, I find it's too bright,
The toaster's in battle, but I'm ready to fight.
The butter's elusive, it sticks to the knife,
I giggle aloud, that's just morning life!

The eggs are now dancing, they jump in the pan,
Whatever I'm cooking, it's part of the plan.
A splash and a dash, oh joy, what a thrill!
With the spice of my laughter, I'm caught in the frill.

Chasing the cat who steals my toast,
We giggle together, I love him the most.
He leaps on the counter, such a little jerk,
In this frolicsome morning, he's such a perk!

With coffee in hand, I hear the day call,
Today is the canvas; let's jump and let's sprawl.
Brushed by the moments, I seize every ray,
In this playground of sunrise, I'm ready to play!

Sunlit Journey

The alarm clock rings, it's still dark outside,
I hit snooze so hard, oh, what a ride!
With pillows as mountains, I conquer in dream,
But sunlight's peeking, it's bursting at the seam.

Coffee cup in hand, I dance on the floor,
The dog skids by, he's opened the door.
With a bark and a woof, he barrels ahead,
I'm giggling and stumbling, but this is my stead!

I grab my old hat, it's got quite the flair,
Sunglasses perched, I'm beyond all compare.
The world awaits with its playful embrace,
I skip down the sidewalk, a skip and a race!

Every step brings joy, a bright sunny face,
With laughter and sunshine, I find my own pace.
This journey is golden, come join in the fun,
Together we'll chase the light; oh, what a run!

Whispered Secrets of the Dawn

The rooster crowed, a funny sight,
A sleepy face, not quite upright.
Coffee brewed, a fragrant cheer,
Another day, wait, where's my beer?

Cats parade with tails held high,
Plotting mischief, oh my oh my!
They prance around, like tiny kings,
Decoding secrets that morning brings.

Giggles spill from mugs of cream,
Grandpa stirs awake from dream.
He cracks a joke, his smile so wide,
Who knew mornings could be this bright?

The sun peeks through with its golden ray,
Chasing shadows, making them sway.
A dance begins, oh what a jest,
Who knew mornings could be the best?

Sunlit Stories

Bacon sizzles, a happy tune,
Flip it quick, or it'll be strewn!
Pancakes stack up, buttery bliss,
Do I smell syrup? Can't resist!

The dog snorts loud, he seeks the crumbs,
While kids play tag, running like bums.
They tumble down, laughter in the air,
Who knew mornings could be so rare?

Birds chirp gossip, such a chatter,
Who wore the best feather, does it matter?
They flit about, bright colors unfurled,
Refreshing tunes in the waking world.

Sunrise stories, nothing but fun,
Embrace the day, the silly has begun.
Every moment, a joyful start,
Each whispered tale, a morning's art.

Early Light Chronicles

The alarm blares loud, hitting snooze,
What a way to wake, good news!
A breakfast blunder, eggs on the floor,
The dog thinks that's a tasty score!

Neighbors wave with sleepy frowns,
A morning stroll in mismatched gowns.
They laugh and joke, what a sight,
Who wears pajamas at eight, right?

The sun climbs up, spilling its gold,
Chasing away the stories told.
Tickled by warmth, giggles abound,
Life's little treasures in moments found.

Muffins rise, just like my mood,
Here's to laughter, it's time to brood.
Every dawn, a comic play,
Who knew mornings brought such display?

The Promise of New Days

The jogger tripped on a wayward shoe,
And laughed it off, oh what a view!
A squirrel stole snacks, a cheeky thief,
Nature's comedy, beyond belief.

Kids splash water, giggles galore,
Sprinklers dance, who could want more?
With lemonade poised, like a king's crown,
Stopping the day from turning brown.

Sunshine winks, teasing the breeze,
Fluttering flags, bending the trees.
Everyone grins, in joy they bloom,
Nothing like humor to chase away gloom.

Chasing shadows, with jokes we make,
Each dawn's embrace, a fresh heartache.
New beginnings, every single play,
Who knew laughter could pave the way?

The Silence Before the Light

The cat snores loudly, dreams of fish,
The alarm clock battles, what a swish!
Coffee's brewing, gurgles with glee,
I'm becoming one with my favorite tree.

A sock is lost, where could it be?
Under the bed, or stuck in a spree?
Birds are chirping, they've made a nest,
Chasing sunrise, oh, what a quest!

Aroma of Possibility

Pancakes flip and then they fly,
Syrup lands right on my tie.
Butter melts in a happy whirl,
My dog drops toast, oh what a girl!

The toast pops up, like it's gone mad,
Butterfingers are something I've had.
Morning smells like cinnamon bliss,
Then I trip on my shoes – that's the gist!

Resurgence at Dawn

Sunrise dances, a cheeky grin,
Coffee spills, let the chaos begin!
A dance with shadows, feet all a-twirl,
I swear I'm having a dizzy whirl.

The cat struts by, tail in the air,
As if he owns all the morning flair.
I chase my dreams; they laugh and run,
But it's harder than trying to catch the sun!

The Parchment of New Light

Sketchbooks open, the ideas flow,
Oh look, there's breakfast, just stole the show!
A pancake tower, high as a cloud,
Syrup waterfalls, I feel so proud!

From the balcony, laughter does bloom,
As breakfast spills onto the living room.
A new day dawning, with giggles and cheer,
Who knew mornings could be this dear?

The Alchemy of Daybreak

The sun sneezed, it's a bright affair,
Coffee brews like magic in the air.
Toast jumps high, a small acrobat,
Butter slinks in, smooth as a diplomat.

Birds gossip loudly, a feathery crew,
While cats plot mischief, in shadows they stew.
Pajamas parade, what a sight to behold,
Life's little circus, so cheerful, so bold.

Mirrors reflect a surreal kind of fight,
With toothpaste battles, morning's delight.
A dance of missteps, a juggle in flair,
In this alchemy, there's laughter to share.

So let's raise our mugs to the morning's delight,
In this whimsical chaos, everything's right!
Waking up's an art, we're all in the show,
Each dawn is a canvas, let's paint it aglow.

The Colors of Yesterday

Yesterday's colors, a bit out of tune,
I spilled orange juice on the floor—what a boon!
Purple socks mismatched with flair and with pride,
Laughter erupts, what a glorious ride!

Green eggs from breakfast? Oh, please, let it slide!
Bacon might sizzle, but it's nothing to hide.
Coffee's a river, it flows like a stream,
As I ponder last night's bizarre, vivid dream.

Chasing the dust bunnies, a whimsical chase,
They hop like little rabbits, it's quite the embrace.
I trip on a shoe, it's a hilarious fall,
Life's colors are vivid in this funny brawl.

So here's to bright moments, both silly and sweet,
Each mishap and giggle makes life feel complete.
Paint today with laughter, let joy take the lead,
And wear yesterday's colors as a badge, yes indeed!

A New Chapter Under the Sun

Under the sun, a new chapter unfolds,
With pancakes that flip like tales yet untold.
Socks on the roof? Oh, what a surprise!
The dog winks at me, mischief in his eyes.

A bubble of laughter floats high in the sky,
As cereal dances, oh my, oh my!
Worms in the garden throw a party so grand,
While ants march on duty, a diligent band.

The broomstick's a horse, let's gallop away,
To a land full of giggles, where we all play.
Frogs croak their wisdom, oh what a delight,
Each page of this chapter is silly and bright.

So let's chase the sun, with smiles all around,
In this bright little world, joy knows no bound.
Write your own story, let humor take flight,
Each dawn is a cue for a laugh, pure and light!

Morning's Gentle Caress

Morning tiptoes in, soft and light,
With yawns that echo through the cozy night.
Pajamas clash as I stumble from bed,
A sock on my foot, another on my head!

Breakfast debates, what shall we consume?
A smoothie or cereal? They both feel like doom.
My hair's a wild creature, with curls that betray,
Yet in this chaos, I giggle and sway.

The world winks at me through a sunlighted gaze,
A butterfly lands, it knows all my ways.
And though I may fumble, I'm bright-eyed and free,
For morning's gentle touch is just magic to me.

So grab that old coffee, let's embrace our own pace,
In this goofy ballet, we've all found our place.
Life's a big puzzle, each piece is a cheer,
In morning's soft caress, we find what we hold dear.

The Aroma of New Beginnings

The toast pops up, a sudden dance,
Butterflies in flight, take a chance.
Coffee spills like morning cheer,
Who knew breakfast could bring such fear?

The cat jumps high, lands in my lap,
A furry tornado, time for a nap.
Wishing the toast would butter itself,
Between sips of life, I'll hide on a shelf.

Socks mismatched, it's my new style,
Dance like a fool, stick out my smile.
Life's little joys, a cheeky parade,
In this quirky start, I won't be dismayed.

Chasing the toast while my pants are gapped,
Laughing at life, I'm freshly wrapped.
So let the day roll, with its silly plight,
In chaos I find my pure delight.

Reflections of Day's Arrival

Awake to the sounds of a loud clatter,
The dog's just messing with my ladder.
Sunlight spills like spilled juice,
Oh, the morning's no time for excuse!

The mirror's reflection greets me with pride,
What's that green thing? Oh, a plant I tried.
With bedhead stylish, I start to strut,
A fashion icon? More like a nut!

Breakfast demands, but pancakes can wait,
While I step on the cat—now that's fate!
Syrup dreams dance in a jiggly swirl,
Just another day in my weird little world.

But as I blink at the calendar's face,
Another day of this wild, wacky race.
With laughter like sunshine filling the air,
Here's to the chaos and moments we share!

Embracing the Dawn

A rooster crows in a very rude tone,
Pancakes and syrup? I'm not alone.
The sun peeks in with a cheeky grin,
Ready or not, let the chaos begin!

Running late, with two shoes unmatched,
Coffee in hand, that's properly hatched.
The kid's drawing tattoos on my arm,
Turns out it's markers—oh, that's the charm!

Sneaky squirrels dance in the backyard,
Plotting their heists? Foraging's hard.
While I prepare for the wildest day,
It's just my family in a wacky ballet.

So, I hug the morning, with laughter abound,
In this delightful mess, pure joy can be found.
With giggles that sparkle like dew on the grass,
I dive into madness—let the moments amass!

Whispers Beneath the Sky

The sun yawns wide, a sleepy affair,
I pour too much creamer in my hair.
Birds gossip loudly from tree to tree,
What's with the drama? Let's keep it free!

A squirrel puts on a show, quite profound,
Bouncing, leaping—all without sound.
I join the performance, twirling in place,
But trip on a toy—oh, what a disgrace!

Dancing in circles as breakfast is made,
The blender screams like it's been betrayed.
Eggs jump on the counter, a clumsy display,
Yet laughter erupts and washes woes away.

So here's to our mornings, where chaos can rule,
With funny little things, we must keep our cool.
Beneath the vast sky, dreams take their flight,
In our whimsical world, everything feels right.

The Sunlit Path Ahead

The sun peeks in with a grin,
It tickles my toes, where dreams begin.
Coffee brews like a magic spell,
Perking up my heart, oh so swell.

Birds sing tunes of a silly dance,
While squirrels plot mischief at a glance.
A butterfly flutters with a wink,
As I spill juice—right down the sink!

The flowers yawn, stretching wide,
While bees buzz with silly pride.
The world awakes, all bright and loud,
As I scurry to join the crowd.

And laughter bubbles in the air,
Like giggles spun without a care.
Each morning brings a fresh new play,
A whimsical start to the day.

The Lilt of Dawn

The rooster crows a cheeky song,
In a world where wacky things belong.
A sleepy cat does yoga on a chair,
As I ponder who cut my hair!

The toast pops up, a crispy cheer,
It's just another day, oh dear!
The cereal dances in my bowl,
While I pretend to take control.

Clouds chuckle as they float up high,
I wave at a duck that's passing by.
The sun plays hide and seek, it seems,
While I trip over my own daydreams.

Joy spills over in every hue,
As I chase my runaway shoe.
The dawn's mischief is plain to see,
Let's laugh and spill our coffee free!

Radiance Rising

Awake with chuckles, birds on cue,
As I trip over my left shoe.
The sun peeks out, a golden ray,
It tickles trees to start the day.

A cloud with bumps floats overhead,
I wonder where it keeps its head?
The breeze tells tales of silly schemes,
Like socks and sandals, fashion dreams.

The flowers nod, they know the drill,
While ants march proudly, against their will.
A wobbly worm takes center stage,
While I giggle at a passing page.

With laughter loud in morning's light,
Every moment feels just right.
In this radiant, whimsical play,
Every dawn ignites a silly day!

Hope's Palette

The canvas of dawn comes splashed with cheer,
A rainbow crew, each color near.
The sun pops up like popcorn done,
In a morning filled with giggles and fun.

A dog barks out a goofy tune,
While I juggle breakfast—yes, with a spoon!
The pancakes flip as they try to fly,
While I just stand and laugh—not shy.

The garden hums with a quirky beat,
As worms dance in the summer heat.
My coffee spills, a painted mess,
Yet in this chaos, I feel so blessed.

With each new hue, my heart takes flight,
In the wackiness of morning light.
This palette of hope brings a silly grace,
Painting joy on life's endless space!

The Ethereal Break

Coffee pot whistles, dance on the counter,
Dancing in slippers, what a great sound!
Toast pops up, like it's got a quirk,
Butter flies high, what a spread, profound!

The cat is plotting, a scheme with a grin,
While I'm still weary, half-lost in a dream.
The sun tickles windows, a cheeky old sin,
And here I am, just trying to beam!

Cereal spills, a colorful mess,
I navigate mornings like a rookie on skates.
With milk in my hair and no time to dress,
I laugh at my chaos—what fun awaits!

So here's to the dawn, a quirky ballet,
Where laughter and blunders turn gray into gold.
Embrace the odd moments, come what may,
For morning's a circus, bit silly, yet bold!

Colors of the Heart

Woke up to rainbows spilling on sheets,
My socks are mismatched, a terrible fright.
Pancakes waving, saying 'Good morning, please!'
While syrup runs wild, a sugary flight.

Neighbors are bickering over a pet,
A duck in the yard? Oh, what a sight!
With giggles and snickers, we place our bets,
'Will it quack or fetch?' Let's enjoy this delight!

A canvas of dreams on the toast so divine,
Buttered morning whispers, 'Let's make a scene!'
The fridge hums a tune like a master design,
While I plan my day with blueberry cream.

So cast all your worries, let colors abide,
In this silly chapter where joy takes its part.
We'll roast the mundane, laughter as our guide,
With every new morning, we paint from the heart!

A Gentle Bloom

Garden's awake, the bees throw a bash,
Daisies are gossiping, petals all aglow.
The sun spills its laughter, a radiant flash,
While plants bend and wiggle, putting on a show.

A squirrel in the tree, with acorns to share,
It's plotting heists while looking so cute.
With warm morning light and everything fair,
I'm struck by the urge to dance in my boots!

The rain might come, but who even cares?
I'll borrow the sun and dance with a grin.
With flowers all prancing, like they're on airs,
Life's little quirks coaxing out all the win!

So here's to the mornings, soft as a sigh,
Where laughter's the fragrance in petals so bright.
Let whimsy and wonder paint every sky,
In the garden of life, we bask in delight!

The Glint of Morning

Sunlight peeks in, like a curious kid,
Bouncing on beams, with mischief galore.
The toaster's a gremlin, popping out bread,
As I trip on my shoelace and tumble on the floor.

Coffee's a rocket, ready to soar,
I taste it too hot but it wakes me with glee.
The clock's in a hurry, and I'm just a chore,
While my hair's an explosion—it's good to be me!

Outfits are wrestling—what can I wear?
Grappling with choices like a circus act.
I finally settle, with flair and with flair,
A mess of bright patterns, that's just how I'm packed!

So greet every morning, with giggles and twirls,
Where absurdities blossom like daisies in bloom.
Life's just a sketch, with ink and with swirls,
In the canvas of dawn, chase away all the gloom!

First Light Reflections

In the dawn, my bed's a trap,
I'm snoozing, oh what a nap!
Alarm rings loud, my senses flee,
Chasing dreams, not destiny.

Coffee brews, my morning friend,
A liquid hug, the day to mend.
With a yawn, I twist and twirl,
Am I awake? Oh, what a whirl!

Slippers on, I shuffle slow,
An obstacle course of doughnut dough.
Birds sing tunes, I can't recall,
Are they mocking? Not at all!

Gazing out, I spot a cat,
Dancing on the fence like that.
Oh, the antics of the day,
Unfold with joy in every way.

The Sun's Embrace

The sun peeks in with a wink,
I spill my drink—oh, how I stink!
Lucky socks, not a pair in sight,
Fashion faux pas from day to night.

Breakfast calls, a burnt toast foe,
Charred and crunchy, oh my, no!
With jelly on the ceiling high,
It's breakfast art, I can't deny.

Outside I trip on fuzz from grass,
A squirrel laughs while I pass.
In this fun, chaotic race,
Who knew mornings had such grace?

The sun waves down, a big old star,
"Time to shine!" it shouts from afar.
I grab my hat and dance along,
In the sun's embrace, where I belong.

Daybreak Serenade

The rooster sings a screechy tune,
While I snooze like a lazyoon.
Pajamas tangled, hair a fright,
Is it morning? What a sight!

The cat, my partner in this game,
Gives the sun a run for fame.
Lazily lounging, she takes her pause,
While I consider my morning laws.

Breakfast mix-up—oops, not a meal,
Last night's pizza? That's the deal!
Cheese and pickle, what a delight,
A culinary joke in morning light.

With giggles and grumbles, the day unfolds,
Stories of mornings, hilariously told.
So join the dance, let laughter sway,
In this wacky dawn's ballet!

The Rise of New Beginnings

Rise and shine, or just roll over,
The bed's so cozy, I'm a true lover.
The blanket wins, I lose this fight,
But here comes sun to set things right.

Out of the sheets, I greet the day,
In slippers, I slide, what can I say?
Oh look, my hair's a wild mess,
A crown of curls in morning's dress!

Toothpaste splatters on my chin,
A minty smile, let the fun begin.
I stumble, fumble, and then I find,
Life's little joys, oh so well-timed.

The day appears with a cheeky grin,
As I'm ready, clumsily, to dive in.
Hold on tight; it's all a show,
With morning laughter, off we go!

The Drift of Morning

The sun peeks in with a cheeky grin,
The dog now barks, let chaos begin!
Coffee's brewing, but I hit snooze,
What's more important? Sleep or news?

Toaster's popping, toast flies high,
I dodge it quickly, oh my, oh my!
Dancing around in pajama pants,
Who needs a plan when you can dance?

I spill some juice, it stains the floor,
The cat just stares as if wanting more.
A cereal mountain, I take a climb,
Breakfast adventure—what a good time!

The mirror's fogged, I look like a mess,
This morning saga, I must confess.
But laughter reigns, as the day unfolds,
In the drift of mornings, life's stories told.

Dawn's Embrace

The rooster crows, with a hey and a ho,
I swear it thinks it's a morning show!
Socks are mismatched, a fashion trend,
Who needs style when laughs never end?

The cat jumps up to steal my toast,
I'm just here for butter, not for a roast!
Coffee spills, providing a scene,
In this funny show, where chaos convenes.

The paper's crumpled, headlines a mess,
A three-legged race to get breakfast!
We sip our drinks, in mismatched cups,
That's how our day really starts up.

With a giggle and snort, we start the run,
Dawn's embrace can't weigh down the fun!
Life's quirks welcomed with open arms,
In each silly moment, we find our charms.

Sunkissed Memories

Sunlight dances on my tousled hair,
The neighbor's dog give me quite a scare!
I trip on shoes left out from last night,
But the world just giggles, oh what a sight!

Breakfast calls, pancakes stacked so high,
I reach for syrup, but why, oh why?
It spills and splatters, a sugary mess,
Dining disasters, our morning's success.

The garden gnomes, with mischievous smiles,
Seem to chuckle as they watch all my trials.
Mismatched garden tools, a gardener's plight,
Yet laughter grows, like plants in sunlight.

These sunkissed moments, filled with delight,
Make the morning mischief all feel so right.
In the heart of chaos, joy's never far,
We shine like the sun, just be who you are!

Serenity's First Light

The first light flares, with a raucous cheer,
The neighbor's radio blares in my ear!
I dodge a lawn chair, trip on some grass,
Oh look, the squirrels—they're up to mischief en masse!

A jogger's out, but I'm stuck in bed,
Cereal boxes piled high, it's chaos ahead!
Milk waterfall cascades down my shirt,
In morning madness, deep down I smirk.

Waking the plants with an accidental spill,
The laughter gathered, it's quite a thrill.
A pancake flyby, they soar through the air,
It's a morning circus, there's joy everywhere!

With a heart full of giggles, I embrace the day,
Serenity's light, in its hilarious way.
With each silly chaos, my spirit climbs,
In the dawn of laughter, life's often sublime.

www.ingramcontent.com/pod-product-compliance
Lightning Source LLC
Chambersburg PA
CBHW051644160426
43209CB00004B/783